T0128018

Worship:
Time in the Word
Worship the Lord in Truth

Evelyn Pettie Reid

Thy word is truth. (John 17:17)
Let the words of my mouth and the medication of my heart
Be acceptable in your sight, O Lord my strength and my Redeemer. (Psalm 19:14)

WESTBOW
PRESS®
A DIVISION OF THOMAS NELSON
& ZONDERVAN

WestBow Press books may be ordered through booksellers or by contacting:

WestBow Press
A Division of Thomas Nelson & Zondervan
1663 Liberty Drive
Bloomington, IN 47403
www.westbowpress.com
1 (866) 928-1240

Scripture taken from the King James Version of the Bible.

Scripture taken from the Holy Bible, NEW INTERNATIONAL VERSION®. Copyright © 1973, 1978, 1984, 2011 by Biblica, Inc. All rights reserved worldwide. Used by permission. NEW INTERNATIONAL VERSION® and NIV® are registered trademarks of Biblica, Inc. Use of either trademark for the offering of goods or services requires the prior written consent of Biblica US, Inc.

ISBN: 978-1-5127-5401-8 (sc)
ISBN: 978-1-5127-5402-5 (hc)
ISBN: 978-1-5127-5400-1 (e)

Library of Congress Control Number: 2016913642

Print information available on the last page.

WestBow Press rev. date: 9/19/2016

Our Magnificent God

Who is like the God we serve? What finite mind can comprehend His greatness or the magnitude of wisdom? We are like a pinion in His vast creation. How blessed are we that He would allow mortal people like us live under the shadow of His wings.

This study of worship and praise has helped me tremendously in my quest to know my God intimately. It is my desire that as you read these pages, you too will have a personal encounter with our great, awesome, and powerful God. May God's peace rest, rule, and abide with you forever as you get to know Him more intimately!

Enjoy,

Evelyn Reid

Contents

Part I

Part II

Foreword

Dr. Donald M. Reid

Larnell Harris, one of the all-time great gospel artists, wrote a poignant song, "I Miss My Time with You." Some of the words are, "I miss my time with you, those moments together, and it hurts me when you say you're too busy!" Life really has become a pressure cooker for many Christians! We are trying to provide for our children and raise godly families, days seem to get shorter, and schedules are crowded, all waging war against our spiritual lives. What we need is to carve out more time to worship and praise God for all the marvelous things He had done for us.

Evelyn Reid seeks to remind, inspire, and encourage us to make more time to be in the presence of our Lord.

This book will help the busy Christian who wants to spend more quality with God! It's not just another book about devotion. Let her take you on a journey toward spiritual renewal and regain your power as you seek to serve and walk with our Creator and Redeemer.

Donald M. Reid

Dedication

This work is dedicated to my mother, the late Martha Ruth Walker Pettie, a great, God-fearing woman who would gather her children and sometimes the neighbors' children and read to us stories from the Bible. On one occasion Mama was reading to me and my siblings the story of Moses and how the glory of the Lord passed by him. Every day Mama would gather us together and before our midday nap read to us the Bible as we sat on the floor and played around her feet. I must have been about four or five years old listening quietly as she read to us the story about Moses. When Mama got to the part of the story where Moses asked God to show him His glory, He did this by passing by Moses and showing the backside Himself. Mama started to cry. As she cried, my older sister Barbara got up and put her arms around her, providing comfort, while the rest of the siblings were caught up in Mama's tears. However, I was confused and didn't know what was happening, so I said to myself, "I don't like that man named Moses because he made my mama cry."

Mama died a few days after her forty-third birthday and left behind a young husband and eleven mostly young children. I was considered one of the little kids. I've never forgotten Mama or her desire to teach God's word us. Many years later in my life I was reading the Bible and I came upon the story of Moses in Exodus 33:18. I too began to cry the same as my mother. Then it hit me! This was why my mother cried. Moses saw God up close and personal. He had a personal encounter with the true and Living God. What an awesome experience for Moses, my mother, and me. What an awesome feeling I felt, the same joyous explosion of spiritual bliss just like Mama.

Although Mama has been in heaven a long time, since 1967, I still remember how she instilled the word of God in me. I thank her for that. She never saw me become an adult, what my daughter looks like, or what kind of woman I would become, but I thank her for praying for me and sharing Jesus Christ with me. I am saved because of her teaching. I am blessed because of her love. I thank you, Mama, for praying for us that God would save all of your children. God answered your prayer that one day all your children would be saved, and we are. There are no words that I can express, no amount of praise I could give to let you know how much I truly appreciate what you did in sharing Jesus Christ with us. My having a relationship with Him is worth more than any gold or silver or any of the world's richest, and for that alone I will love you forever, Mama.

I'm grown now, a mother, a pastor's wife, and a grandmother. I still have many of the qualities you taught me as a child. I am still your little star child and the same little girl you called Teediecat. Someday I will see you again. Thank you for teaching me how to walk in His love and pointing me in the right direction. Thank you for the legacy you left all of your children.

Your loving daughter,

Evelyn Maxine Pettie Reid (Teediecat)

In Loving Memory of:

My loving parents, Dana B. Pettie and Martha Ruth Pettie;
My beloved sister and brother,
Monica Schneal Moyer and Patrick O'Neal Pettie;
My sweet and loving niece, Little Miss Trekeyta Nicole Nibblett;
My kindhearted and loving sister-in-law, Earnestine Pettie;
My wonderful brothers-in-law, James P. Holland,
Valeiger Seay, and Kennon Shelton;
My adorable father-in-law, John William Reid (JW);
My friend Miss Angela Smith;
and last,
Dr. Willie L. Reid Sr., our dearly beloved and truly missed uncle.

May the peace of God, which passes all understanding,
rest with you as you rest in His love and peace.

Special thanks to Dr. Donald M. Reid, my husband, who loves me and always encourages me to do my best. He proofreads my work and makes many helpful suggestions to help me improve upon my weakness and writing skills. To Leni Shontae' Wilson, my daughter, a teacher who holds a master's degree in education. I call her princess, and she teaches me how to listen and encourages me along the way and also offers me helpful insights on my work. I especially want to thank God for my grandson, Evan Donald Simmons, who brings me joy every time I see his face. To McKenzie Seay, my goddaughter, who keeps me on my toes. To Eric Manson Jr., whose kindness and love are always present in his love for me. To my family of Martinsville, Virginia, I love you guys. To the Aletheia Baptist Church family, who supports me richly, thank you. May God bless you real good. Words cannot express how much I appreciate your loyal support, help, and encouragement. To Mrs. Shirley Williams, who helps me by proofreading and correcting my many mistakes. And last but not least, my former pastor, Dr. Lehman D. Bates, Yvonne Barts of Ft. Washington, Maryland, and Burrie and Sheryl Pinnix. These are my friends, who love me and encourage me and remain my friend in spite of all my shortcomings. Thank you so much, and I love you always.

The Reason for This Book

While thinking about my life and watching the world take a downward spiral spiritually, I wanted an up-close, personal, and intimate relationship with my Lord and Savior Jesus Christ before taking my journey home to heaven. In my quest to know Him better, I wanted an in-depth look at how to worship and praise Him. What I discovered has amazed me.

Being no expert in scriptures, yet I have learned that if you take some time to know Him, He will give you more insight into who He is. He is a great God who is full of mercy and truth. This study has caused me to see the Lord in a different light with a closer view of who He is. This work started from a simple desire to know God better. I did not want to leave this world without knowing the God of the heaven in a more intimate way.

My prayer is that as you take time to read this study material, you will be rewarded greatly with more kingdom knowledge of God.

Be blessed and enjoy,

Evelyn Reid

Part I

Worship Is an Encounter with the Living and Holy God

One day Moses was tending the flock of his father-in-law Jethro, the priest of Median, he went deep into the wilderness near Sinai, the mountain of God. Suddenly the angel of the lord appeared to him as a blazing fire in the bush. Moses was amazed because the bush was not engulfed in flames, but didn't burn up. Amazingly, Moses said to himself, why isn't that bush burning up? I must go over to see this." When the Lord saw that he had caught Moses's attention, God called to him from the bush, Moses, Moses! Here I am, Moses replied. "Do not come any closer, God told him. Take off your sandals, for you are standing on holy ground." Then he said I am the God of your ancestors the God of Abraham, The God of Isaac, and the God of Jacob. When Moses heard this, he hid his face in his hands because he was afraid to look at God. (Exodus 3:1–6)

Today, if you had an encounter with the holy and living God, would you know it? Would you fear and revere Him? In this passage, we see Moses doing his daily task of tending to his father-in-law's flock. Notice where he was: He was deep in the wilderness, which means that he was away from family, friends, and the daily distractions of life. He was in a position to hear. He was aware of his surroundings, with his ears and eyes open, and he was paying attention to his environment.

How many of us go through life and never see or experience the benefits of the quietness of our surroundings? Moses was not only in a quiet place, but he was in a holy place—the very mountain of God. The mountain of God is a place where His glory and presence are located. It is a place of sweet serenity. It is a place of beauty and rest from a weary day. It is a place of reverential awe because of the awesomeness of God. It is a place where His awesomeness can never be penned into words. And it is a place of gentleness, where one can encounter the presence of the living God.

This is what Moses did. When the angel of the Lord (the preincarnate Christ) appeared to him in a blazing fire in a bush, Moses was amazed. In other words, he was curious. There was something about that burning bush that caught his attention and curiosity. Moses's curiosity wouldn't let him just walk away. Instead, he moved toward what he was seeing. He wondered why that bush wasn't engulfed in flames.

If modern-day believers had an encounter like Moses, would they stop, look, listen, and turn to pay attention, away from the world's distractions? Would their curiosity lead them in a direction that would allow them to know if God was calling them for a divine purpose? Or would their schedules be so bombarded with their own agendas that God's plan would have to be put on the back burner?

When the Lord saw that He had caught Moses's attention, He called to him from the burning bush. Would you know if God was calling you? Would you know and trust Him no matter what the circumstances are? If the Lord called your name, would you answer?

When the Lord called Moses, he answered, "Here I am." Moses heard the Lord's call and answered. Moses was on his way to get closer to the unconsumed burning bush, but the Lord stopped him by calling his name and giving him instructions. "Don't come any closer; take off your sandals, because you are standing on holy ground."

The Lord identified Himself to Moses, letting us know that the God of the universe wants us to know Him and wants to be close to us. This reminds me of the scripture that says, "Draw near to me and I will draw near to you" (James 4:8).

I am the God of your ancestors; I am the God of Abraham, the God of Isaac, and the God of Jacob. Moses knew who He was and whom He was talking about, because Moses identified with his forefathers—Abraham, Isaac, and Jacob. When Moses heard this, Moses hid his face in his hands because he was too afraid to look at God. Moses had a connection to his past, for he knew who his ancestors were and what they stood for. What they believed had been passed down for generations. It's too bad that many of our children and grandchildren are not aware of the rich traditions of our faith—the struggles and testimony of a rich heritage.

My question today is, are we afraid of God, and do we fear Him? If we were summoned to His presence today, would we recognize His voice and follow Him?

Oh Lord, please allow us to be mindful of Your presence in our lives today, and give us the strength to answer Your call if we are summoned. Help us to come closer to You in order to know You better. Help us to be humble and respectful. Help us to walk in the light of Your word and recognize Your voice when You speak. Grant us Your peace, and show us today what You would have us to do.

My Prayer

Dear Lord,

Let me stop and pay attention to the unconsumed burning bushes in my life. Help me to be quiet so that I can hear Your still, small voice. Help me to sense Your presence and know for certain that I am there. Let me hold my peace and keep silent when You are giving me instructions. Help me not be blindsided by the distractions of this world. Let not the noises of this world fog my mind and ears, that I fail to be in Your presence, because too much of the world has taken residence in my life. Help me find the time to spend time with You daily. Forgive me of all of my shortcomings, and keep me in Your perfect peace. Amen!

My thoughts:

_____
_____
_____
_____
_____

What I learned from this chapter:

_____
_____
_____
_____
_____

How can I apply what I learned from this chapter?

_____
_____
_____
_____
_____

My prayer:

_____
_____
_____
_____
_____
_____
_____
_____
_____

Worship Is Reserved for God Alone

You must worship no other gods, but only the Lord for He is a God who is passionate about His relationship with you. (Exodus 34:14)

How awesome and incredible is the God of the universe—a God who is passionate about a relationship with us. He cares for us and wants to welcome us into His presence. He invites us to spend time with Him and teaches us wonderful and beautiful things about Himself.

Through His word He allows us a look into the indescribable beauty of His in-depth plan for our lives. He also allows us see a glimpse of the things He has prepared for our future. He encourages us to walk through the valley of the shadow of death without fear. He protects us with His wings like a mother hen protects her baby chicks from a raging storm.

The Lord leads us in the right path and protects us from our enemies. He gives wisdom, and He corrects us when we are wrong. He is a light to our path and shows us the dangers so we can walk the distance in comfort, in peace, and without fear.

He provides laughter and teaches us how to eat, drink, and be merry with what time He has allotted us on this dash through His universe. He allows us to see that there is glory in His presence and that He will keep us in His perfect peace—so long as we keep our minds focused on Him. God's wisdom is great and mighty, and He rules in ways that are too wonderful for us to grasp.

No matter where we are, God is there, and I have confidence in what He has ordained for my life. His mercy is endless, and His grace is sufficient for the plans He has for me. As I survey God's word, I can see why King David was called a man after the Lord's own heart, because he kept his mind and his heart tuned in to God's Word.

My Prayer

Dear Lord,

Let me never forget or try to get past knowing that You are the only true God and that there is no other God besides You. Forgive me for my independence, thinking that I can do anything without you. I know that it is because of You that I am able to live, move, and have my being. No matter where I go or how I search, there is no one greater or more powerful than You. I revere You, bow down to You, and respect You more each day as I learn of your grandeur; I know that I am just a drop in the bucket. Thank You, Lord, for seeing this little drop and making me something special in Your eyesight. There are no words of understanding that can describe how great You are. My life is in Your hands, and I thank You for this. Thank You for Your daily presence. Please be with me today, and let me be mindful of Your daily presence. Thank You for caring for me with Your outstretched arms. Lord, it is You who keeps me safe and protects me from my enemies. Let me be one after Your heart. Correct me when I am wrong, and show me great and marvelous things in Your Word. Let me love others as You have loved me. Allow me to follow in Your footsteps as I journey from the earth to heaven. Please help me keep in view eternity; let it be in my mind and close to my heart on a daily basis. Let me be solely dependent upon You for my daily provisions. Thank You, Lord, for letting me know beyond a shadow of a doubt that You are the only God and that You are passionate about Your relationship with me. Amen!

My thoughts:

_____
_____
_____
_____
_____

What did I learn from this chapter?

_____
_____
_____
_____
_____

How can I apply what I learned from this chapter?

_____
_____
_____
_____
_____

My prayer:

_____
_____
_____
_____
_____
_____
_____
_____
_____
_____

In Worship, We Ascribe to the Lord the Glory Due to Him

Give honor to the LORD, you angels; give honor to the LORD, for his glory and strength. Give honor to the LORD for the glory of his name. Worship the LORD in the splendor of his holiness. (Psalm 29:1–2)

Oh Lord, how great you are. You are worthy of all of our praise, honor, and devotion. Who is like You, Lord, and what mortal can give You the entire honor You deserve? It is only through what You have revealed that we have a glimpse of how powerful, great, and awesome You really are. My little vocabulary cannot ascribe the magnitude of Your splendor.

It is a privilege to know what little I know about You. If I studied all day and night, I still could not grasp the wonders of who You are. How mighty and devoted You are to the world You created. You are special and kind for all the beauty and the wonders of this great world You made for Your children to enjoy and spend their time on the earth. You gave us the sun, moon, and stars. You gave us the seas and the land. You gave us free and fresh air. You put eyes in our heads so we could see our way and feet to go in any directions we choose. You gave us all kinds of food for the nourishment of our bodies. And You gave us a body properly designed to live in the environment of the earth. You gave us seasons and times of fellowship and the ability to procreate and bring forth life.

Oh Lord, forgive us that we have not honored You and given You the glory You fully deserve. Forgive us for not worshiping You in the splendor of Your holiness. Forgive us for our greed of taking what You have given freely and putting a price tag on it. Forgive us for putting down another brother or sister who has been created in Your image and calling them out of the name that You called them. Forgive us of the sin that has reigned in our mortal bodies since Adam sinned in the garden. Forgive us of living independently of

You. Lord, we know that You are merciful and kind, and we need Your kindness to live in us today.

My Prayer

Dear Lord,

Let me honor You with my mouth and with my actions until You call me home. Forgive me for lack of knowledge in Your word. Let me be forever mindful and grateful of what You have shown me in Your word. Help me to know and tell others of Your goodness and mercy. Let the rest of my life be wrapped up, rooted, and intertwined with You. Let me not look to the right or to the left and not trust in the knowledge of man above Yours. Lord, You are the only true God, who knows all things and the only one who is worthy of all our praise, honor, respect, and love. Help me keep my mind stayed on You. Amen!

My thoughts:

_____
_____
_____
_____
_____

What did I learn from this chapter?

_____
_____
_____
_____
_____

How can I apply what I learned from this chapter?

_____
_____
_____
_____
_____

My prayer:

_____
_____
_____
_____
_____
_____
_____
_____
_____

We Can Worship Because of Christ's Sacrifice on Our Behalf

The old system in the Law of Moses was only a shadow of the thing to come, not the reality of the good things Christ has done for us. The sacrifices under the old system were repeated again and again, year after year, but they were never able to provide a perfect cleansing for those who came to worship. If they could have provided perfect cleansing, the sacrifices would have stopped, for the worshipers would have been purified once for all times, and their feeling of guilt would have disappeared. But just the opposite happened. Those yearly sacrifices remained them of their sins year after year. For it is not possible for the blood of bulls and goats to take away sins. This is why Christ, when he came into the world, said, "You did not want animal sacrifices and grain offerings. But you have given me a body so that I may obey you. No, you were not pleased with animals burned on the altar or with other offerings for sin. Then I said, Look, I have come to do your will, O God, just as it is written about me in the Scriptures." (Hebrews 10:1–10)

Christ said, "You did not want animals sacrifices or grain offering or animals burned on the altar or other offerings for sin, nor were you pleased with them" (though they were required by the Law of Moses). Then He added, "Look, I have come to do your will." He cancels the first covenant in order to establish the second. And what God wants is for us to be made holy by the sacrifice of the body of Jesus Christ once for all times.

My dear and wonderful Lord and Savior, how blessed I am that I have eyes to see Your word and ears to listen to what the Holy Spirit is teaching me about You. Words cannot be described to mortal men what You did for us when You said that You had come to do God's will. Forgive us that we take Your death lightly, as if it was something of old and unimportant. But the truth of the matter is what You did by sacrificing Yourself; You gave us eternal life through Your precious and valuable blood.

Thank You that I didn't live under the law of Moses because if I had to bring an animal sacrifice each year, I probably would have never done it, because of my fear of the animals and the blood would terrify me. You came and took away that fear and the responsibility of searching out an unblemished offering. Your sacrifice made it easy for people like me who are fearful of animals to come to Your throne of grace and receive the mercy and grace You give freely to those who receive Your Son.

Thank You that You foreknew and understood people like me and that You made it possible for people like me to be saved. Forgive me, Lord, for all of my past sins when I didn't know about You or the perfect sacrifice You made for me in Your Son, Jesus Christ. Thank You for making a new or second covenant and removing the old law, and thank You, Jesus, for Your obedience. Had You not been willing to make that sacrifice, the entire world may have been lost. Just understanding and knowing this makes me know why we will all bow down to worship You. You are truly worthy of all praise, honor, and glory.

You are a giver, and we are constantly taking without ever stopping and counting the cost of the sacrifice You made for us. We take, we eat, we enjoy Your world, and many of us fail to give You thanks, glory, and honor. Because of what You did for us, we ought to stay on our knees and shout from the mountaintops how great and awesome You are.

We should never allow false or pagan little gods stop our praise for You. Those who know You should speak in one voice. Our God is one God, and He alone rules this world. He is worthy of our praise, and we ought to honor Him with our lips, our sacrifices, our money, our love, our reverence, and with all of our being. Thank You, Lord, for the sacrifice You made for me by laying down Your life and giving Your precious blood and dying on the cross for us.

We are a chosen people, a royal people, that our Savior would love us so much that He would give His only Son for us.

My Prayer

Dear Lord:

From this day forward, let what You did for me on the cross be forever in the front of my mind and in my heart. Let me never forget. Keep my total being stayed on You, and let me be rooted and intertwined with You in my daily walk through Your world. Let me see the beauty of Your creation in every step I take, and give me Your peace as I survey the wonders of Your creation and the beauty of Your word. Let me come to You for comfort, and let me ask You for my daily bread. When I see Your creation and all that You put in it, including man, remove my blinders, and let me always see Your hand and Your love. You are merciful even in my storms, and when I trust You, I rest in Your peace. You, Lord, are beautiful to me, and I never want to underestimate who You are in my life. Keep Your hand upon me, and let me be a light in Your world. Amen!

My thoughts:

_____

_____

_____

_____

_____

What did I learn from this chapter?

_____

_____

_____

_____

_____

How can I apply what I learned from this chapter?

_____

_____

_____

_____

_____

My prayer:

_____

_____

_____

_____

_____

_____

_____

_____

We Should Worship with Reverence for God

Since we are receiving a kingdom that cannot be destroyed, let us be thankful and please God by worshiping him with holy fear and awe. For our God is a consuming fire. (Hebrews 12:28)

Thank You, God, for salvation and the inheritance we will be receiving when we get to heaven. What You are giving us cannot be destroyed. You are worthy and deserved all honor and glory. Lord, I want to please You in all areas of my life. The eyes of Your children have not seen or comprehended all that You have in store for us who love and honor You.

You are like a fire shut up in my bones that can't be put out. Pleasing You is the reason for my existence. You know the plans You have for me, plans for my good and not for my disaster. Your plans will give me a future and hope (Jeremiah 29:11). It was only in my quest to know You that I could learn Your word intimately, to know You more completely and live my life holy by keeping the promises You have graciously given. Then my life would blossom and be fruitful for Your kingdom.

You are the God of true forgiveness, the God who is there to help us when we cannot see our way. As You were there with Moses at the crossing of the Red Sea, You are there for us, for it was there You showed all who were with him, including his, enemies how great and powerful You are. You are a great and mighty God who has prepared a place in eternity for those who have trusted Your Son and love and obey Your word.

Lord, because of the mighty kindness You have shown to us, let us move forward knowing that You are guiding us in the right direction. Let us not grow weary in doing well and not faint on our journey. Let us continue to look to the hills from where our help comes, and when trouble is at our door, let us count it as joy when our faith is being tested.

Lord, You know all about us and how we will act when we are suffering. Please allow us to rest and realize that You are still in control even when we can't see the outcome. When the storms of life are raging and we don't know how we will make it through the night, let us be confident in knowing from Your word all that You have done for us, and to trust You no matter what our end results may be. Thank You for preparing a place for us that can never be destroyed.

Let us move forward, knowing that Your promises are true and that even in the midst of our troubles and struggles You already know the outcome. Help us to reach out and touch You as Peter did when he walked on water. When Peter called Your name, You answered the call. When the storms of life are raging, we know that You can calm our storms by speaking a word. Let Your word be settling in our hearts, minds, and souls that no matter what kind of lemon the world offers, You are there to help us make it lemonade.

Lord, You are right in all Your ways. How wonderful it would be if the people who are called by Your name would humble themselves and pray and if the praying warriors of the world would pray the kingdom of darkness right out of this world. How awesome this world would be.

Lord, be near me always, and let me not drift away from following after You. Let me know You in a pure and perfect way. Cast my iniquities far from me, and wash me white as snow. I have sinned and come short of Your glory and Your holiness. Let my time here on earth honor, love, and obey You in all areas of my life. You are good, and Your mercy is everlasting. Let me rest in Your arms and be comforted as a newborn baby rests and depends on its mother. When I am overwhelmed, keep me calm. When I am disobedient, discipline me. When I have doubt, teach me to trust You, and when trouble has surrounded me, let Your will be done in my life. Let me live so You can use me anywhere and anytime.

Lord, I don't know what You are doing in my life, but You do, so let me trust in You with all my heart, soul, and mind.

My Prayer

Dear Lord:

Keep me close to You. Don't let me look away from You. Hold my hand as I walk through the journey You have prepared for my life. When my life is over, let my work on earth come forth as pure gold. Forgive me of my sins, those known sins and those that only You know. Search my heart and know me, and show me any wickedness found in me. When my wickedness is revealed to me, help me seek Your guidance that will lead me in a direction where I can be washed. Let not the life I am living be in vain and unfruitful. Show me great and mighty things in Your word. Thank You for preparing a place for us that cannot be destroyed, and please be a consuming fire in my life. Consume me and fill me with Your word. Let the word that I have hidden and planted in my heart come up and grow, that I may lead others to be a part of Your kingdom family. Help me to lead someone to You today. Lord, I thank You for the privilege of worshiping You. I love You, Lord. Amen!

My thoughts:

_____

_____

_____

_____

_____

What did I learn from this chapter?

_____

_____

_____

_____

_____

How can I apply what I learned from this chapter?

_____

_____

_____

_____

_____

My prayer:

_____

_____

_____

_____

_____

_____

_____

_____

_____

When We Draw Near to God He Draws Near to Us

Draw close to God and God will draw close to you. Wash your hands, you sinners; purity your hearts, you hypocrites. (James 4:8)

How can I draw close to God and know Him personally? How can I clean up myself to walk upright with the Savior of the world? How can He love me with all the sin I have committed since my birth? How can God love me so much that He gave His only begotten Son, Jesus Christ, to cover my sins? How merciful is Jesus that He forgives my iniquities and washes me with His precious blood? Why is Jesus so humble and loving?

I don't have the answers to all these questions, but I do know that it was God who chose me before the foundation of the world and that His organized plans were so different from my plans, for in my plans I never factored in God's plan for my life. I was moving at a fast pace, following my own advice, taking my own actions, by directing and charting the course that I wanted for my life and in my own way. Even though I had Christian attached to my name, I was lukewarm. I had no personal relationship with the Savior of the world, nor did I understand the need to have Him in my life. And I definitely didn't have plans for Him in my future. I was off and running, blind as a bat, and following an agenda that could have been life threating.

But Father Time stopped me in my tracks, and I found myself in a whirlpool of a messed-up life. I was afraid and a prodigal, too much pride to ask for help. Even in that lowly state of my life while running away from God and God's people by hiding in the dark speckles of life, out of desperation, I called on the name of the Lord. He heard my cry and welcomed me back into His arms and still loved me as His child. How fearful I was, how painfully sick I was, how weary my soul was, and how my choices had led me astray and down a path of destruction. I had to come to the folk in the road, and I had to choose a direction in my life. My first choice was like

Lot of Genesis, I chose the plush green grass, the watered fields, and the lights of the city. After getting there, I found it wasn't green grass after all; it was only AstroTurf. There were many heartaches and many undesirable times of frustration and pain. I had chosen the wrong path and was headed on a course of action that would not only destroy me as a person but would also cause me to lose my soul. I only had a form of godliness, but I had no personal relationship with God. When I cried out, He heard me and came to my rescue and gave me what I needed most.

The God of heaven sought after me and found me in despair He cleaned up my wounds, gave me a change of clothing, and washed me white like snow. He forgave me and cast all my sins as far as the east is from the west. He established me and raised me up so I could walk on mountains and stand of the stormy seas without doubt or fear. He gave me a new name, new hope, and planted a desire in me to know His Word. He gave me a new beginning and made His name great in me. He took me, a nothing, and nobody, one who had no hope in life, a middle child from a large family, and He blessed me and saved me and causes me to draw close to Him and live under His protection.

Oh Lord, I love You, and I trust You with my life. You have healed me and saved me and gave me hope. Let me draw close to You every day. And if I drift away, reach out with Your loving arm and bring me back to the safety of Your arms and Your love. Grant me daily the portion of life You have for me, and never let me wander into the wildness of life without taking You with me. When my heart wants to play with the world, send Your angels and block me. Speak to me just as You did to Balaam in the Bible when You spoke to him by the mouth of a jackass. Watch over me, and show me great and wonderful things from Your word.

How majestic You are, oh Lord, for the world and all that is in it belongs to You. Help me to be mindful of Your presence, and let me ask for Your advice. Help me to wait and be still while I am waiting for Your answers.

My Prayer

Dear Lord,

Draw close to me and stay with me forever. Let me draw close to You by learning Your Word and keeping what I learn in my heart. Let Your steadfast love lead me by allowing me to be obedient to what You teach me. Let me do great and marvelous things for Your kingdom, and let me not embarrass You or cause You to be ashamed of me. Let me forever lean and depend on You, and let me rest in Your will for my life. Help me to accept what plans You have for me, and let me do what is necessary to fulfill all that You have planned for my life. Let me see You and see You in others. Let me be mindful that all people are created in Your image and in Your likeness and that You have created them for Your purpose and not my agenda. I want to grow and be more like You as I walk in the footprints You have placed before me in Your word. Let me be faithful and stay rooted down and filled to the brim with Your Word. Keep me faithful today and every day by allowing me to lead a soul to the saving knowledge of Jesus Christ. As I draw near to You, may the words of my mouth and the meditation of my heart be acceptable in Your sight. Lord, please hear my prayers and discern what my heart needs, for only You can keep me and watch over my soul, keeping me until the day You call me home. Amen!

Evelyn

My thoughts:

_____
_____
_____
_____
_____

What did I learn from this chapter?

_____
_____
_____
_____
_____

How can I apply what I learned from this chapter?

_____
_____
_____
_____
_____

My prayer:

_____
_____
_____
_____
_____
_____
_____
_____
_____
_____

Come and Worship

Come, let us worship and bow down. Let us kneel before the Lord our maker, for his our God. We are the people He watches over, the sheep under His care. Oh that you would listen to His voice today. (Psalm 95:6–7)

Come! You have been summoned to the house of worship, and when you get there, you are to bow down and kneel before the Lord, our Maker, because of who He is. He is our God. We are the people He watches over. In other words, He keeps his eye on us at all times. We are the sheep under His care; He is our shepherd who protects us and keeps us from all hurt, harm, and danger. He knows the dangers in our path, and He protects us as we walk blindly down a cliff or into a world that will utterly destroy our lives. Who am I that the mighty God of the universe, the Creator of heaven and earth, is mindful of me and keeps me under His all-powerful, all-seeing, and all-knowing watch.

The Lord is good and is worthy of my honor, my respect, and my praise. I will come to Him with singing in my heart and praise on my lips, for He is the one who created me and gave me His breath of life. Without Him I could do nothing.

Have you been summoned to the house of worship, but you chose to stay home at Bedside Baptist? Do you not care that the King of the universe has invited you to His throne room? Are you too proud to kneel and bow down before your Maker? Do you know who you belong to? Have you harden your heart so you cannot hear the midnight cry to come and fellowship with Him? He has summoned us to come into His presence to worship Him in all of His glory and splendor. Do you know Him as your personal Savior, and does He know you? If He called your name, would you answer? Would you know His voice, and could you turn the world loose so you could come to Him and become His disciple?

When we come to worship the Lord, He protects us and conceals us, and He hides us from the troubles and dangers in our path. He takes us and places us on a high rock out of the reaches of our enemies. The Lord will work out all things for His good and according to His purpose and His plans for our lives. For He is a never-changing God, a God of love and mercy, and His faithful love will endure forever.

The Lord is King, and we will worship Him with gladness. We are to abide in His word daily. When we abide in His word daily, His word abides in us. We need not be ashamed of rightly dividing the word of truth. His word becomes a lamp to our feet and a light in our path. His word is truth and is never failing.

Because we belong to Him, we know Him because we study His word and meditate on it day and night. Therefore, we delight in the teaching of His word. He is the one who is the Shepherd over His word, and His word does not go out void, but it takes root in us and it grows.

Softly and tenderly His voice is calling us. Don't harden your heart or run from the call. Today and every day God is bidding us to come to Him. He wants you to heed His call, lay down all weight, and things that do not pertain to the voice of the living God. He is waiting; all you have to do is answer the call.

So today as you heed the call to come and worship, put on your running shoes and run quickly to the voice of the Almighty and bow down before Him and give Him some of your valued time. He is waiting with open arms. Even if you are a prodigal son/daughter, He is still standing there with open arms ready to welcome you back and celebrate with you because He knows the one who was lost today has now been found.

Come home! He is calling you today.

My Prayer

Dear Lord,

Thank You for looking beyond my faults and seeing my needs. Thank You for giving me the wisdom to listen and hear Your voice. Thank You for allowing me to be aware of Your voice and aware when You are calling me out of my worldly life into a life of Your marvelous grace and mercy. Live in me, and let my life reflect Your holiness. Let my home become Your home and be a place where Your glory dwells.

Oh Lord, when I hear Your call, let me run toward Your goodness and mercy, and let me not run in the opposite direction. Thank You for inviting me into Your family. Be with me today, and let all who see me today rejoice in the good You have done for me. Let me lead a lost soul to Your kingdom. Thank You for all of Your blessings, in the precious name of Your Son, Jesus Christ. Amen!

Your daughter,

Evelyn

My thoughts:

_____

_____

_____

_____

_____

What did I learn from this chapter?

_____

_____

_____

_____

_____

How can I apply what I learned from this chapter?

_____

_____

_____

_____

_____

My prayer:

_____

_____

_____

_____

_____

_____

_____

_____

_____

_____

In Worship We Know Who We Are in Christ Because We Are Warned in His Word

Jude a servant of Jesus Christ and brother of James, to those who have been called, who are loved by God the Father and kept by Jesus Christ; Mercy, peace and love be yours in abundance. (Jude 1:1–2)

Do you really know who you are in Christ? If asked, could you tell somebody about your personal relationship with the King of the universe? Do you know Him? Do you have an understanding of who He is? If He were to come into your presence today, would you recognize anything about Him? Are you saved, and if you are, can you explain it to others? Some of us are attached to a denomination, a church name, or even a pastor. But today I want to share with you some of the facts that are presented in the book of Jude.

It is my hope that this devotional moment will cause to you to want to carefully examine who you are in Christ Jesus and if necessary, change your direction so you may understand your eternal destination. It is also my desire for you to turn to God's word and study it for yourself.

First, we must know who we are and what we believe. We are Christians. Christians are Christlike people who follow the ways and teaching of our Lord and Savior Jesus Christ. We are believers, who believe that the Bible is the inspired word of God, the written record of His supernatural revelation of Himself to man, absolute in its authority, complete in its revelations, final in its contents, and without any errors in its teaching (2 Timothy 3:16–17, Matthew 5:17, 2 Peter 1:20–21).

The book of Jude is only one chapter, and you could probably read it in one sitting and in less than ten minutes. My desire for you is for you to grasp some wonderful and lasting knowledge in knowing who you are in Christ. I pray that you will study to show yourself approved as you grow abundantly in His grace and mercy.

Those Loved by God
As Christians We Should Know (Jude 1:1b–3)

1. You have been *called*
2. You are *loved by God the Father*
3. You are *kept by Jesus Christ*
4. We *share* the same *salvation*
5. We are to *contend* for the *faith* that is *entrusted to the saints.*

What great love the Father has for those who love Him and those who are loved by Him. His word is clear and leaves us with much testimony of how much He loves us. God called us before the foundation of the world to be His chosen vessels. He loved us and gave us His Son, Jesus, to keep us. Then He let us know through His word that we share the same salvation. This means that no matter where you worship, if we believe what the Bible teaches about His Son, Jesus Christ, we share in the same salvation. This is good to know, because now we don't have to tear down others who don't worship in our local congregation. God has His followers all over the world who have not bowed down to the corruption of this world. To believers, this means that we can now defend the faith that is entrusted to us His saints. Because the world if so full of so much ungodliness, it will take all believers to fight for what we believe and know is right. We cannot afford to let any of the godlessness that is in the world creep into the church. We must not sit silently by while Satan puts his little leaven of poison into the minds and hearts of our congregations.

We know by the word of God that many false teaching are out in the world. Those who know God must be mindful of their surroundings and be on guard to keep what God has entrusted to them from being polluted with the ungodly teaching of this world.

This is why we have the warning in God's word, so that we can know and be aware of the craftiness and deceitfulness of Satan.

The Reason to Be on Guard (Jude 1:4)

1. Certain men have secretly slipped in among you.
   a. They are godless men.
   b. They change the grace of God into a license for immorality, and they deny Jesus Christ, our Sovereign and Lord.

We know that godless men and women exist today. We also can see the wickedness that is in the world being displayed in every marketplace where all can see the shame, which lies in our hearts. What use is it to be right, which is now considered wrong? The world is taking on an "everybody does what is right in their own eyes" attitude.

The Lord: A Reminder of Who God Is and Who Men Are Who Have No Understanding (Jude 1:5–10)

1. The Lord will deliver and destroy.
2. He delivered the people out of Egypt but later destroyed those who did not believe.
3. The angels, who did not keep their natural position of authority but abandoned their own home, these He has kept in darkness, bound with everlasting chains for judgment on the great day.
4. In a similar way Sodom and Gomorrah and the surrounding towns gave themselves up to sexual immorality and perversion. They serve as an example of those who suffer the punishment of eternal fire.
5. Dreamers, who pollute their own bodies, reject authority and slander celestial beings.
   a. These are men who do not understand truth.

    b.   They are men who speak abusively against whatever they do not understand and what things they do understand by instinct, like unreasoning animals. Those are the very things that destroy them.

In light of what we know about our God, we are to be mindful of the sins that so easy beset us. We are to be on guard for what we allow to come into our homes, our presence, and into the lives of our children. We are to know that God is watching us and delivers us from many things. Yet, He will also punish unbelief and wickedness. Therefore, be on guard, watch, and wait patiently for our Sovereign Lord, for He will return and will reward His faithful saints.

Their Fate: You Reap What You Sow (Jude 1:11)

1. Woe to them they have taken the way of Cain
2. They have rushed for profit into Balaam's error
3. The have been destroyed in Korah's rebellion

Choose your path carefully, because we cannot hide anything from God. We should consult the Lord and wait for Him when we are planning our future. What may seem to be the right path may be the wrong one, and the enemy may be waiting to destroy your life. It is best to stay on the straight and narrow path that leads to eternal life than to be on the path that leads to destruction.

Who They Are? They Are Among Us (Jude 1:12–13)

1. These men are blemishes at your love feast.
2. They eat with you without the slightest qualm.
3. They are shepherds who feed only themselves.
4. They are clouds without rain, blown along by the wind.
5. They are autumn trees, without fruit and uprooted, twice dead.

6. They are the wild waves of the sea, forming up their shame.
7. They are wondering stars, for whom the blackest darkness has been reserved forever.

When looking around, you would never think to observe acquaintances, family, friends, and church family as possibly being used by Satan. Some of the people we love and trust are the last ones we would consider that have sold out to Satan in order to bring us down.

Enoch Prophecy about Such Men (Jude 1:14)

1. The Lord is coming with thousands of His holy ones

As sure as the world exists, the Bible declares that the Lord is coming again not as the Lamb, but as the Lion. He will judge the deeds of men.

Their Job (Jude 1:15)

a. To judge everyone
b. To convict all ungodly acts done in an ungodly way and of all the harsh words ungodly sinners have spoken against Him.

Be mindful that there will be an end to all ungodly living. We all have to give an account of ungodly acts, ways, and words spoken against God.

What These Men Are Accused Of (Jude 1:16)

a. They are grumblers
b. They are faultfinders
c. They follow their own evil desire

d. They boast about themselves

e. They flatter others for their own advantage

We know that we are living in the last days because of the teaching of God's word. The Bible is clear in its teaching that in the last times, there will be scoffers (those who are characterized by their own selfish lust and who follow their own ungodly desires). These are men who divide you. They create factions in the church following their natural instincts and do not have the Spirit. These are men who are clearly not saved. They are ungodly and false teachers.

In Light of This Knowledge: What the Church Should Do (Jude 1:20–23)

a. Build yourself up In the most holy faith.

b. Pray in the Holy Spirit.

c. Keep yourself in God's love as you wait for the mercy of our Lord Jesus Christ to bring you to eternal life.

d. Be merciful to those who doubt.

e. Snatch others from the fire and save them.

f. Show mercy, mixed with fear.

g. Hate even the clothing stained by corrupted flesh.

The word is clear what Christians ought to do, look, and be like. We are living in difficult days. The world looks like it is winning the battle. But God promises us the He is able to keep us from falling and to present us before His glorious presence without fault and with great joy. He is the only God our Savior, with glory, majesty, power, and authority, through Jesus Christ our Lord, before all ages, now and forevermore. Our God is an awesome God.

We all have skeletons in our closets and have done some things that have grieved the Spirit of God. But thanks to God that in His mercy He sought us, saved us, and gave us a new life vastly different for the old one!

My Prayer

Dear Lord,

Thank You for snatching me out of sin and darkness and pointing me in the direction of Your light and love. Help me to always be mindful of Your presence in my daily walk. You are good, and Your mercy endures forever. Forgive me of all my sins, known and unknown. Let Your light shine in me, and let all who meet me today will know that I have been in Your presence. Thank You for loving me enough to pull me away from eternal damnation and putting me on the right path. You are my God, and I am Your child. Grant me wisdom to know You better. I love You!

My thoughts:

_____
_____
_____
_____
_____

What did I learn from this chapter?

_____
_____
_____
_____
_____

How can I apply what I learned from this chapter?

_____
_____
_____
_____
_____

My prayer:

_____
_____
_____
_____
_____
_____
_____
_____
_____

In Worship, We Know How to Treat the People of God

Dear friends, you are faithful in what you are doing for the brothers, even though they are strangers to you. They have told the church about your love. You will do well to send them on their way in a manner worthy of God. (3 John 1:5)

How do you treat God's people, especially the men of God? Do you show hospitality? If God showed up at your doorstep today, how would you treat Him? Would you treat Him with leftovers or give Him your best? Or would you know that He was God in person?

The believer's role in the church is to show hospitality to all and especially to Christians, and men of God, and to praise them for their service (3 John 1:1–7).

Gaius is addressed as a friend whom is loved.

a. There is a prayer to enjoy good health and that all would be well with his soul.
b. Gaius is commended for his faithfulness to truth and his Christian walk, which gives John great joy.
c. Gaius is praised for helping strangers, sending them away in a manner worthy of God.
d. Believers are to show hospitality to men of God so that the church can walk together in truth.

Exposure of evil leaders in the church: the church should know and mark men like Diotrephes, a church leader who was evil. Here is what he looks like (3 John 1:9–10).

1. He wants to be important.
2. He will have nothing to do with others in the church.

3. He gossips maliciously about other leaders.
4. He refuses to welcome brothers to the church.
5. He stops those who want to do so and puts them out of the church.

Evil leaders ought to be exposed in the church. In fact, if they are sowing discord among the brethren and causing some to turn away from following after the teaching of the Bible, God's word, they not only need to be exposed but excommunicated from the children of God. This teaching may seem harsh, but the Bible is clear in showing us "a little leavens the whole lump." If there is an infectious cancer in the body, it needs to be addressed. Otherwise that little lump will become huge and eventually affect the whole congregation. My desire for you is that God's words penetrate your heart and take up residence in your life. May God's peace be with you and me.

My Prayer

Dear Lord,

Keep my mind stayed on You, and don't let the little foxes of the world cause me to stumble and fall. Keep Your eyes set upon me, and let me not turn from following after You. Clean me up and make me ready for my journey home to Your joy. Let my life here on earth reflect Your goodness and kindness. Let me be hospitable to all I come in contact with, and let me treat all who enter my abode with the fruits of the Spirit. Dear Lord, make my home Your home, and let all who enter feel Your presence. Thank You, Lord, for saving me, loving me, and being in my life. You alone are worthy of all my praise. Amen!

My thoughts:

_____
_____
_____
_____
_____

What did I learn from this chapter?

_____
_____
_____
_____
_____

How can I apply what I learned from this chapter?

_____
_____
_____
_____
_____

My prayer:

_____
_____
_____
_____
_____
_____
_____
_____
_____
_____

Be on Guard: Watch out for Deceivers, for They Are Among You

Many deceivers, who do not acknowledge Jesus Christ as coming in the flesh, have gone out into the world. Any such person is the deceiver and the antichrist. (2 John 1:7)

In this modern age with so many distractions and things to do that do not pertain to our Christian life, it makes it hard to conceive that in our everyday world there are deceivers living among us. It is so hard to pinpoint what a deceiver looks and acts like. The only way to know who or what they are can only be found in the word of God. That's why studying your Bible daily and spending time in prayer and with other believers who have a like mind-set is the only way to know what you are dealing with.

In this study John is teaching us how to be on guard for our lives and how to watch out for deceivers who will try to destroy us. This teaching shows us what a deceiver and an antichrist is. If you were confronted with a deceiver, would you recognize him? Could you call out a deceiver on the carpet if necessary? Can you tell the difference between a true born-again believer and a deceiver? Do you know that a deceiver comes in all colors? Have you shown someone from the word of God what a deceiver is? Do you know what truth is?

Today as we look at this study, let's begin by looking at truth first.

The Salutation to (2 John 1–3)

1. The Chosen Lady and her children
   a. They know the truth.
   b. They love the truth.
   c. The truth lives in us and will be with us forever.

  d. Grace, mercy, and peace from God the Father and Jesus Christ, the Father's Son, will be with us in truth and love.

How good is it to see your children walking in the truth and in the light of God's Word? Many have raised children who have brought shame and heartaches to the family. Many have raised children to become great success stories in the world. But it is nothing like raising a child to be useful in the kingdom of God. The question is, what you are raising your child to be? At the end of their lives, will they thank you that you gave them a good, solid foundation in the truth of God's Word? It is my hope that if you give to your children a biblical base worldview of God, and that what you are teaching them, will lead them on a straight and narrow path that will lead them to eternal life.

The Commendation (2 John 1:4)

2. I have great joy knowing that some of your children are walking in the truth just as the Father commanded us.

Can you as parents and grandparent feel the joy of leading your child in a direction of kingdom living? If not, isn't it time to get busy? It is never too late to lead the ones you love to salvation. It is our duty, and we will not regret it in the long run if we don't do it. How good and pleasant it is to see and know that our children and grandchildren are walking in the ark of safety and serving God.

Exhortation and Warning (2 John 1:3–11)

The reason I am writing:

3. To ask that we love one another
  a. That we walk in obedience to His command
  b. To walk in love

Are you walking in obedience to God's commands? Do you love your fellow man? If you were to come face-to-face with your Creator, would you have the confidence that you have been obedient in His command to walk in love? I know you say there are some people who are too difficult to love, and we all experience a few people in our lives who are totally hard to love unconditionally. What should we do? We must first seek God's wisdom on how to love those unloving people in our lives. Pray for them, and keep them in your prayers always. Don't let Satan deceive you by telling you that you just can't love that person. Remember, that person you are having a hard time loving just maybe your test.

Why?

4. Because many deceivers do not acknowledge Jesus Christ as coming in the flesh.
   a. They have gone out into this world.
   b. Any such person is a deceiver and an antichrist.
   c. Watch out. Be on guard that you do not lose what you have worked for, but that you may be rewarded fully.
   d. Anyone who runs ahead and does not continue in the teaching of Christ does not have God.

Do you have God? Are you on guard at all times? If you met a deceiver, would you recognize him? That is why the word of God is so important, because the word teaches us how to know what a deceiver is and to be mindful of what an antichrist looks like. You can only know this for yourself if you can identify him through the word of God. Let God's word speaks to you as you study and apply God's word to your daily walk.

Knowing Who You Are

5. Continue in the teaching.
   a. But whoever continues in the teaching has both the Father and the Son.
   b. Anyone who do not bring this teaching, do not take him into your house or welcome him.
   c. Anyone who welcomes him shares in his wicked works.

So based on what you've learned today, will you be able to know a deceiver? Will you continue in the teaching about the Father and the Son? Who are you listening to? Have you compared what they are teaching to the scriptures, and if not, why are you welcoming them into your home? Those you welcome into your home for teaching purposes, are you sure they are teaching the pure, uncompromised word of God? Stay focused and guard your heart and the hearts of your children. Satan is actively trying to get his paws into your children and lead them away from following after God. His is a master deceiver, and his job is to rob, kill, steal, and destroy us. Keep your heart, your mind, and your soul protected and saturated with the word of God.

My Prayer

Dear Lord,

As we learn Your word, let us walk in the truth. Let us not be caught up in every wind or doctrine that comes our way. Let us be swift to hear but slow to speak, and let us know the difference. Let us not be easily misled, and keep us in Your care. Thank You for choosing me and putting me in a position where I can hear and learn Your truth. Let me be mindful of my surroundings and know and follow truth when I hear it. May Your peace be upon us all. Amen!

My thoughts:

_____

_____

_____

_____

_____

What did I learn from this chapter?

_____

_____

_____

_____

_____

How can I apply what I learned from this chapter?

_____

_____

_____

_____

_____

My prayer:

_____

_____

_____

_____

_____

_____

_____

_____

_____

_____

God's Children Are to Walk in Light and Love

Those who obey his commands live in him, and he in them. And this is how we know that he lives in us: We know it by the Spirit he gave us. (1 John 3:24)

Jesus is the Word of life, and Jesus is the light of the world. Jesus is the way, the truth, and the life, and no one come to the Father but through Him. Finding that great light is like finding a precious and valuable stone whose untold riches are more valuable than anything our finite minds can imagine or comprehend. To obey His commands means that God's love is made complete in us.

Would you know the light if it showed up in your presence right now? Are you sure you know God? But more importantly, are you sure that He knows you? Saying we know and love God, whom we have not seen, and hating our brothers and sisters, whom we see every day, may be our hint to check our lifestyles to see if we are on the right path to our eternal destiny.

How do you know love when you see it? We know love by this, *that He laid down His life for us; and we ought to lay down our lives for the brethren* (1 John 3:16). Is there anyone you know that you would lay down your life for? Now pause and think about that. I know for myself I'd have to pray hard and long to carry out such a task. But that's just what Jesus did for us; He gave up His life for ours. He took us out of the marketplace of slavery and paid our sin debt and set us free. He loved us and wanted us to live our lives free from the sin that so easily beset us and takes us down the road of eternal damnation.

How great is our God that He laid down His life for me and made room for me in His kingdom. Being that God sent His Son Jesus to pay my sin debt, He took my name from the Book of Life and placed it in the Lamb's Book of Life, which guarantees me a place in His kingdom. Lord, I am so thankful for Your great sacrifice for me. You personally chose me, who was nothing, and You made me something in Your eyes. You called me royal, and You gave me an inheritance in Your kingdom. It doesn't matter what the world says or thinks about me; it only matters what You think and know about me.

It is strange that You did not ask of me an unattainable task, for me to be saved and enter Your kingdom; You only asked that I believe in the name of Your Son Jesus Christ and love one another, just as You commanded us to. You made it easy, yet I make it hard by my disobedience.

My Prayer

Thank You, Lord, for what You did for me on the cross. My mind never could have conceived what Your death would mean to me, my salvation, and the salvation to the entire world. Your sacrifice is too wonderful and awesome for me to comprehend what You did for me and how honest and special and loving You are. Lord, You laid down Your life for me, because You wanted me to be with You in Your kingdom. Thank You, Lord, for caring for me in such a marvelous and special way. May I never forget and remember daily that I am bought with Your blood and paid for at a valuable price. May I forever rest in Your love and abide in Your word. May my life and my words be filled with the wisdom of Your word, and may I show others the love You have shown to me. Let not my tongue ever cease from praising You or giving You glory, and let me walk in the light of Your word and of who You are. Thank You, great King and Lord of this world, for Your great sacrifice for me and the people of Your world.

My thoughts:

_____

_____

_____

_____

_____

What did I learn from this chapter?

_____

_____

_____

_____

How can I apply what I learned from this chapter?

_____

_____

_____

_____

My prayer:

_____

_____

_____

_____

_____

_____

_____

_____

_____

Lord, Show Me Your Glory

Then Moses said, "I pray you, show me Your Glory!" (Exodus 33: 18)

Can a mortal man ask of the just and living God, the King of glory, the creator of the universe, the King of Kings, Lord of Lord, and the Lion of Judah, to show him His glory? Moses did, and how could he? How could he approach the God of heaven and ask Him such a question?

Moses could ask such a question because he knew the Lord spent much time in his presence. He knew Him up close and on a personal basis. He sought the Lord for answers as to how to lead His people. When the people became obstinate, the Lord expressed His anger to Moses by saying:

Go up to a land flowing with milk and honey; for I will *not* go up in your midst, because you are an *obstinate* people and I might destroy you on the way. (Exodus: 33:3)

At this point you might be asking yourself what are obstinate people. After finding out, you might even see yourself as an obstinate person. The word *obstinate* as described in the *Oxford American Desk Thesaurus* is an adjective meaning stubborn, mulish, pigheaded, headstrong, willful, perverse, refractory, recalcitrant, contumacious, unmanageable, inflexible, unbending, immovable, intransigent, intractable, uncompromising, persistent, persevering, pertinacious, tenacious, dogged, single-minded, relentless, and unrelenting.

This suggests that the Lord knows us and that He sees our inner parts. He knows our hearts and our thoughts. He knows our personality well and is familiar with the good and evil lurking in us. He is the all-powerful, all seeing, and all-knowing God who is in the midst of His people. Even though the Lord was displeased with the children of Israel at this point, He did not destroy them.

This shows His grace and His mercy and that He is longsuffering and tenderhearted toward us, giving us a chance to get it right.

How sad it is when the God who created us doesn't want to be in our midst. What a fearful thought, that our God for one moment would rather stay away from my presence or have to think about what He wants to do with me. Dear Lord, please don't leave me, and please, give me a heart to follow after You.

For the Lord has said to Moses, say to the sons of Israel, you are an obstinate people; should I go up in your midst for one moment, I would destroy you. Now therefore, put off your ornaments from you, that I may know what I shall do with you. So the sons of Israel stripped themselves of their ornaments from Mount Hored onward. (Exodus 33:5–6)

This suggests that the people had made themselves ready to enter the Promised Land their way. They had made themselves ready by being dressed in what they thought was their best, all decorated in their fancy ornaments. When the Lord saw them, He must have been disgusted with what He saw. They had placed around their necks ornaments of decorative embellishments like frills, trinkets, whatnots, doodads, and various kinds of accessories. The Lord said, "Should I go up in your midst for one moment, I would destroy you. Now therefore, put off your ornaments from you, that I may know what I shall do with you."

Could you strip yourself of your ornaments, things that you see as valuable, things that are popular, and things that may give you status in the world? Would you give them up to follow after God? Young man, could you pull up your pants, and young lady, could your change your vile mouth and move away from those in your life whom you know God is displeased with? Have you put on ornaments, or have you put on the whole amour of God? Only you know where you stand with the true and living God.

And again Moses did just that. Not only did Moses put away, but he moved his location.

Now Moses used to take the tent and pitch it outside the camp, a good distance from the camp, and he called it the tent of meetings. And everyone who sought the Lord would go out to the tent of meeting which was outside the camp. (Exodus 33:7)

Some of us are in a comfortable place in our lives, and it is hard to leave our comfort zone. Would it be hard for you to go outside of your normal activities to meet with God? Would you be willing to go to a place called the tent of meetings and meet with God?

Sometimes in order to hear the voice of God, we must take steps that move us into the presence of God. Sometimes we must leave father, mother, sister, and brother and all other weights that so easily beset us by keeping us from the presence of God. To be a follower of Christ sometimes calls for change. Just as the disciples left their fishing nets and families, we too must be like the disciples and follow Christ. We must put away things that occupy our minds, bodies, and behavior, and we begin by leaving them behind us and pressing toward the mark of a higher calling, turning our backs on the things of the world and turning toward the true and living God.

Whenever Moses entered the tent, the pillar of cloud would descend and stand at the entrance of the tent; and the Lord would speak with Moses. … The Lord used to speak to Moses face to face just as a man speaks to his friend. When Moses returned to the camp, his servant Joshua, the son of Nun, a young man, would not depart from the tent. (Exodus 33:9–11)

How are you when you enter your place of worship? Do you feel like you have been in the very presence of the Lord? Does the Lord meet you there? Did He speak to you through His word? Did you understand His voice and His direction? Moses had a personal relationship with the Lord, and when the Lord spoke, Moses heard. He listened intimately, and he obeyed His voice.

Do you hear His voice, and if so do you obey? These are questions only you can answer, and only you know where you stand with the God of the universe. What an awesome thought it is to know that Moses, a created being like me, got a chance to be up close and personal with the only true God. It is good to know that His thoughts are not my thoughts and His ways are not my ways and that He is concerned about me.

If I could be like Joshua, would I remain at the tent even after the man of God, Moses, left? Would I be close enough to hear the voice of God as He spoke to Moses? Would what I hear draw me close, in hopes that the Lord God would give me a small portion of what He had given Moses? All I know is that Joshua became a great leader after the death of Moses. It makes you wonder if his sitting at the door of the tent where the pillar of cloud descended, did Joshua have an encounter with the Lord also? Even though the Bible does not say at this point, it still makes me wonder.

Moses talked to God face-to-face and reminded God of His words that He had spoken to him about finding favor in His sight. Moses then asked a question and a favor of the Lord.

Now therefore, I pray you, if I have favor in your sight, "let me know your ways that I may know you, so that I may find favor in your sight." Consider too, that this nation is your people." (The Lord spoke) And He said," My presence shall go with you, and I will give you rest." Then Moses said to Him "if your presence does not go with us, do not lead us up from here. For how then can it be known that I have found favor in your sight, I and your people? Is it not by your going with us, so that we, I and Your people, may be distinguished for all the other people who are on the face of the earth? (Exodus 33:13–17)

Do you know God? Could you question Him on the promises He has made with you? Do you respect Him? Do you know Him well enough that you could boldly go to the throne of grace without feeling that God would immediately cut you down? Have you found favor in the Lord's sight? Do you believe and rely on His word? Do you trust Him?

Moses had that kind of relationship with the Lord of glory. He trusted what the Lord said about him, that he had found favor in His sight. Moses made a request of the Lord, *"Let me know your ways that I may know you."* Do you know the Lord, and can you ask of Him to let you know His ways and believe that He would answer you? From what I can see, God wants an up close and personal encounter with His people. When you trust Him, come close to Him, spend time with Him, and ask of Him, He will answer.

God answered Moses by telling him "My presence shall go with you, and I will give you rest." When God tells you something, you can bank on it. It is a done deal! God stands on His word, and He will perform all the promises in His word when we obey Him and ask according to His will. The time of Moses's life was exciting because you can see the presence of God directing Moses's life. Ever since Moses's encounter with the Lord on Mt. Sinai, Moses knew that there was only one God. Moses had a powerful testimony, and just by studying his life we are rewarded the great benefit of seeing the awesome power of the living God. To know that the God of the universe came down to show Himself to one man, Moses, gives me great confidence that I too can have a personal relationship with Him if I trust Him, obey Him, and live my life seeking His face and His plans for me.

Moses talked with God, restating what he had understood the Lord to say and by going a step further by saying, "Is it not by Your going with us?" Your going with us will distinguish us from all the other people on the earth. Moses's question invoked the Lord's response, and the Lord said, "I will do this thing which you have spoken; for you have found favor in My sight, and I have known you by name."

Have you found favor in the Lord's sight? I believe that God wants a personal relationship with us, and He wants to lead us in the path of righteousness. He is with us at all times, and He lives within us daily. Call upon the name of the Lord, and He will answer. Are you listening?

Then Moses said, I pray you, show me your glory. (Exodus 33:18)

Who is this mortal man who approaches the King of the

universe and asks of Him to reveal his glory? Moses had had an encounter with the Lord on Mt. Sinai, and it was there that Moses learned the greatness of God, the Creator of the ends of the earth. Moses obeyed the voice of the Lord, and the Lord had shown him great and marvelous things. Moses listened to God and felt that he knew God and God knew him. He knew of His greatness, and he observed God doing wonders and miraculous things. He had been up close and personal with God when he was given the Ten Commandments. He watched and saw what the Lord did with Pharaoh and the parting of the Red Sea. He watched as the death angel came through Goshen and passed over all homes that had the blood on their doorposts. He knew God was good, and he knew that God would keep His promise to the children of Israel. He had seen more of God than any other man on the face of the earth, and now he wanted to see His glory.

It is amazing what God said to Moses when he asked Him to show him His glory. He did not shun Moses or make an excuse; He came right to the point and was very candid about what He said to Moses. God did not hesitate to tell Moses what He would do. I wonder if we asked God to show us His glory what kind of answer or reply would He give to us.

And he said, I will make all my goodness pass before thee, and I will proclaim the name of the Lord before thee, and I will be gracious to whom I will be gracious, and will show mercy on whom I will show mercy. And he answered, you cannot see my face for there shall no man see my face and live. And the Lord said, Behold there is a place by me and thou shall stand upon a rock: And it shall come to pass, while my glory pass by, that I will put thee in a cleft of the rock, and will cover you with my hand while I pass by, and I will take away mine hand and you shall see my back parts, but my face shall not be seen. (Exodus 33:19–22)

Can your mind comprehend what Moses did and how bold he was in his approach to the Lord of the universe? Do you think that you could ever ask God such a question and expect Him to answer?

But the Lord did just that for Moses. It seemed like the Lord was humbled by Moses's question, and He replied quickly. Could it be that the Lord wants a personal encounter and relationship with His children? It seemed to me like the Lord made a special effort to tell Moses who He was, and He wanted him to know His goodness and mercy. Then He answered Moses's question, letting him know that he could not see His face and live. But He let Moses know that there was a place by him, a rock. That's letting me know that God was near Moses all the time. Do you know if God is near you? Can you say for sure that He is in your midst and will answer you if you call?

Moses asked a bold question, and the Lord answered. The Lord told Moses where to stand and what He was going to do and that He was going to allow Moses to get a peek of His glory. Can you imagine when the Lord's hand covered Moses face, how his heart must have been pounding to know that the Father was that close? But the awesomeness of the removal of His hand and Moses saw His back part. Moses's racing heart must have leaped for joy, and all praise within him must have come to life because the God of the universe had a personal encounter with a mortal man. Have you had that kind of experience, and would you be able to stand knowing that the very Creator of who you are had a personal encounter with you?

Our God is an awesome God, and He is everything and more of whom He has revealed in His word. I am like Moses now; I want to know my Lord and Savior even more. Taking a closer look at the life of Moses and his personal encounters with the God of heaven and earth changes how I think and look at the Old Testament and the great respect I now have for Moses. God is good and wonderful and kind, and there are not words in my vocabulary that could describe the greatness of who I now know our God is. It pays to study God's Word; it pays to know Him in a personal and up-close way. How great and awesome You are. May my experience of learning of Your glory let my face light up like Moses with all my encounters from You from this day forward. Thank You, Lord, for showing and revealing Your greatness to a mortal man and how You have given us a glimpse of who You are and shown me Your glory through the eyes of Your servant Moses.

My Prayer

Lord, thank You for Your servant Moses. Thank You for showing him Your glory. Thank You for allowing Moses the insight to write the first five books of the Bible and allowing me to have more insight into Your person. Lord, I want to be up close and personal with You. I want to know You for myself, and I want to be in a position to always see Your glory in my life. You are my life, and without You I can do nothing. May all who share in this worship study be blessed, and may each one have their own encounter with You. Thank You, great King our Lord and Savior, for being a very up-close and personal God, one who always has our best interest on Your mind and in Your heart. Thank You for having a plan and a purpose for my life. Let my desire always be to follow after You. You are my God and I am Your servant. Use me for Your glory.

Always in His care,
Evelyn

My thoughts:

_____
_____
_____
_____
_____

What did I learn from this chapter?

_____
_____
_____
_____
_____

How can I apply what I learned from this chapter?

_____
_____
_____
_____
_____

My prayers:

_____
_____
_____
_____
_____
_____
_____
_____
_____
_____
_____

Thinking of You, Lord

My Prayer

Lord, lead me in Your righteousness as I go along my way today. Let my heart be filled with love and compassion for Your people as You have shown love for me. Protect my heart, guard my mind, and allow Your servant to be equipped with Your armor of strength.

Let Your word be the strength of my life and my conversations. Let me be mindful of those who will come into my presence today. If by chance You send an angel my way, let me treat him as if You walked into my path. Make me aware of those who have authority over me, especially my husband and friend who watches over my soul. Let me never forget that You are God and You alone rule the universe. Let me find kindness even for those who hate me and kind words for those who do evil things against me.

Forgive me for all my petty ways. Give me the strength to overcome all the little irritations that hinder me from being all that You want me to be. Help me to keep silent when I think I want to speak. Help me to listen and be attentive to someone who may need me to hear them. You know that listening is a real problem for me and that I run my mouth too much. Please bridle my tongue, so that when I do speak, I will only speak what You have laid on my heart.

Help me to bring joy to a hurting heart and strength to someone who is weak. May I never do anything to embarrass You or Your kingdom. May Your peace dwell in my heart today. Lord, let Your glory radiate in my being today. Amen!

Thanks for the Little Things

Lord, thank You for the little things like cleaning my kitchen or brushing my teeth or even being able to feed myself. So many times when I was very sick and unable to do my housework, someone else was doing my housework for me, which made me sometime feel helpless and a teeny-weenie bit jealous. I don't know why, because my house was cleaner then than I could ever have cleaned it even on a good day.

Forgive me for my shortcomings, and help me to always remember how You send us a ram in the bush, especially when we need some tender love and care. It is sometimes hard to let others love us. However, I thank You, Lord, for having those special people in our lives who fill in the gaps for us when we are down.

Thank You for the small things we take for granted each day, like taking a bath, hot running water, and showers that let the warmth of the water flow over us and refresh us. So many days during my illness, I couldn't bathe myself, but You made a way for me and had a ram there for me. Thank You for Beverley Wimberley, who cared for me so lovingly while I was ill and at my worst point. Her kindness and never-ending energy gave me the opportunity to relax and rest and not worry during my illness. Thank You, Lord, for giving us what we need when we need it. Thank You for Beverley. Beverly, I will cherish your friendship and love for all eternity. Words can never express how much I love you and appreciate you.

Life is so special and filled with so many small blessings. We would never have recognized Your grace and mercy if You, Lord, didn't give us a chance to stop, lie down, and have time to pay attention to the tiny details of everyday life. Every life has some kind of trouble or disappointment, but most people don't find it or see the small, unnoticed miracles that happen to us every day.

Dear God, You are good, and You are more than words can express. Thank You so much for Your Son, Jesus, who came to free me, and died for me by laying down His life for the sin of the world. Jesus came to redeem us from a burning hell. You are so awesome, more than my words could explain. You are more than my heart could express. Without a doubt, You are God and there is no god besides You. You alone deserve my praise.

I love You, Lord.

My Prayer

You, dear Lord, are in my thoughts today. Today is a new day that the Lord has given me to be faithful. Yet every day when I allow my mind, heart, and soul to wonder, I find that I am not so faithful after all. Sometimes I allow little distractions, such a phone call, where my curiosity gets the best of me and I find myself listening to the party on the other end gossip or complain about someone in the body of Christ. I find myself participating in behavior that may cause me to drift away by taking my eyes and mind off truth and getting involved in hearsay by saying something I may regret later.

Today as I examine myself, I wonder why so many Christians are so full of envy and strife against one another. Some of the faithful workers in the body of Christ usually work hard and get burned out by those who are not working. They find themselves complaining regularly about the ones who are not fulfilling their duties and vice versa. These are those Christians who are always finding fault in what's getting done and what is not, or they are the complainers who could have done a better job. My question is, "Why don't You do or not do what You are complaining about?"

Lord, I am humbled by what You have allowed me to learn about You. When frustration comes my way, I know that You are in control and that Your plan for me is a much better than any plan I can have for myself. Thank You, Lord, King of the universe, that Your plans for those in our past can help us shape our future and that Your grace and mercy run deep in our history and are even greater in our future.

My Prayer

It is my prayer that all who read this little devotional will see the God of the universe as the only true and living God and that all will turn to Him and trust Him for salvation. May God richly bless You and keep Your in His care.

Worship the Lord in the Splendor of His Holiness

Ascribe to the Lord the glory due his name, bring and offering and come before Him. Worship the Lord in the splendor of His holiness. (1 Chronicles 16:29)

When we worship our God, we are to assign to Him the glory that is due to His holy and righteous name. How can we do this? We do this by loving, admiring, and respecting Him. God our Creator deserves our adoration, devotion, and respect. We must adore and marvel at the great things He has done for us.

We do this by telling all nations what He has done. We are to shout from the mountains, letting the world know how great and awesome our great and powerful God is.

We are to sing to Him, sing praises to Him as we tell of all His wonderful acts. We are to glory in His name and let the hearts of those who seek Him rejoice. We are to look to the Lord and His strength and seek His face always. We are to remember the wonders He has done. We are to remember His miracles and the judgments promised. Knowing that you are His servants, descendants of Israel, His chosen ones, the children of Jacob, we are blessed through His seed. (Who is Jesus Christ?)

He is the Lord our God, whose judgments are all in the earth. He remembers His covenant forever, the promises He made for a thousand generations, the covenant He made with Abraham and the oath He swore to Isaac. He confirmed it to Jacob as a decree to Israel as an everlasting covenant. "To you I will give the Land of Canaan as the portion you will inherit." It is the Lord our God who said, "Do not touch my anointed ones and do my prophets no harm."

Sing to the Lord, all the earth, proclaim His salvation day after day. Declare His glory among the nations, His marvelous deeds among all people.

For great is the Lord and most worthy of all praise; He is to be feared above all gods. For all the gods of the nations are idols, but the Lord made the heavens. Splendor and majesty are before Him. Strengths and joy are in His dwelling place.

Ascribe to the Lord, all you families of the nations, ascribe to the Lord glory and strength. Ascribe to the Lord glory due His name; bring an offering and come before Him. Worship the Lord in the splendor of His holiness. Tremble before Him, all the earth! The world is firmly established and cannot be moved.

Let the heavens rejoice, let the earth be glad; let them say among the nations, "The Lord reigns." Let the sea resound and all that is in it. Let the fields be jubilant, and everything in them! Let the trees of the forest sing. Let them sing for joy before the Lord, for He comes to judge the earth. Give thanks to the Lord, for He is good His love endures forever. Cry out, "Save us, God our Savior; gather us and deliver us from the nations that we may give thanks to Your holy name and glory in Your praise." Praise belongs to the Lord, the God of Israel, from everlasting to everlasting. Then all the people said, "Amen and praise the Lord."

How are you praising God? Have you looked at the wonders of His word? Have you made Him a part of your daily life? Do you publicly give Him glory and honor? Is He the Lord of your life?

What are your filling your life with daily? The soap operas, Oprah, the *CSI* programs, *Scandal*, and *The Good Wife*? Are you giving yourself your daily portions of God's word? Is your telephone, your computer, your children, or a special friend taking up all of your time? Are you giving God your creator any of your time or attention? If not? Why not? Don't you know that people who know their God do prepare as if they are going to die today? Someday we will all stand before God and give an account for the life He has entrusted us with. Don't you think it is time to get to know the God of the Bible? Seek Him now, learn and know His word, and pray for yourself and those who will come after you. Don't let your life come to an end, and you don't know your Creator. Heaven is real and so is hell. The only way to heaven is the trust the Lord and Savior Jesus Christ. Confess with your mouth (that you are a sinner), and believe in your heart that Jesus it the only way to the father. And ask Him to come into your heart and save you and He will.

Romans 10:9 says, "If you declare with your mouth, Jesus Lord and believe in our heart that God raised Him form the dead, you will be saved. For it is with your heart that you believe and are justified, and it is with you mouth that you profess your faith and are saved. As Scripture says, anyone who believes on Him will never be put to shame."

My Prayer

Dear Lord, save Your people today, and let those who are Yours not wonder in the wildness and not find You. Help us to know that it is our duty as Christians to bring people to Jesus and develop them to Christlike maturity so that they will be able to walk in Your way and lead others to You. I pray, Lord, that we Christians will get busy leading sinners to You and that we will wrap ourselves in Your word so that the world may get a good glimpse of You. Keep me faithful and in Your care. Teach me how to serve You and where I am lacking, and shower me with Your mercy and grace. Help me to be a blessing to Your kingdom, and let me never shame You. Praise Your name forever.

Watch over me,
Your child, Evelyn

Part II

Praise More Time in the Word

Behold, I am coming soon, bringing my recompense with me, to repay each one for what he has done. I am the Alpha and the Omega, the first and the last, the beginning and the end. Blessed are those who have washed their robes, so that they may have the right to the tree of life and that they may enter the city by the gates. (Revelation 22:12–14)

Jesus is coming.
Get ready.
Give Him glory.
Give Him praise.
Worship Him.
He is the great I Am.

His is to be what you Him to be, at the hour
that you need Him to be whatever.

Praise

This is my God, and I will praise Him.

Praise! What is it, and why do we need to do it? Praise is to have admiration, commendations, approval, acclaim, to give tribute, applause, to compliment, to give recommendations, to worship, to honor, to have adorations and devotion, to give glory, to have celebration, to give blessings, to give thanks for, to admire, to commend, to extol, to give honor, to complement, to eulogize, to congratulate, to applaud, to hail, to pay tribute to, to glorify, to worship, and to adore. And who in the universe will pay all these tributes to and to give glory to a name? None other than Jesus Christ, who is our Lord and Savior—a name above all other names, one who rules and super rules the universe. Jesus Christ the one who was, who is, and who is to come. He is the one whom will be crowned King of Kings and Lord of Lords. To Him, we bow down; we worship and give glory, praise, and worship alone.

I will sing to the Lord, for he has triumphed gloriously the horse and the rider he had thrown into the sea. (Exodus 15:1b)

Thus the Lord saved Israel that day from the hands of the Egyptians, and Israel saw the Egyptians dead on the seashore. Israel saw the great power that the Lord used against the Egyptians, so the people feared the Lord, and they believed the Lord and in His servant, Moses. There is power in praise. Do you praise the Lord, and if you do, how often? Every praise in our in our heart, mind, and mouth belongs to the Lord. We cannot move, breathe, or have our being without the Lord.

The Steadfast Love of the Lord

Shout for joy in the Lord, O you righteous! Praise befits the upright. (Psalm 33:1)

Our God is a God of grace, and He has given us grace (that is underserved favor) in spite of our sins and shame. Our God has made all things and rules over all things and is worthy of the praise of all people. Because of Him we move, breathe, and have our being. He is a God of love who desires the entire world to be saved, yet He is a God of judgment who will not judge the righteous with the wicked. He is full of mercy, which is compassion, pity, forgiveness, kindness, sympathy, humanity, understanding, generosity, leniency, benevolence, forbearance, grace, blessing, relief, kindness, and peace.

Because of all of these attributes as righteous people, it is our duty to praise the Lord because praise befits the upright, and the upright will give Him praise and honor because those righteous and upright people who know their God will do great exploits.

Taste and See That the Lord Is Good

I will bless the Lord at all times His praise shall continually be in my mouth. (Psalm 34:1)

The faithful understand the goodness and the greatness of the Lord. They understand that His plans will be successful. Because of who He is, we know that His protections will always be with us and we can trust Him no matter what storms come our way. It ought to be the intention of all saints to bless the Lord at all times and let our praise of Him be continually in our mouths and thoughts always. His word teaches that He will keep us in perfect peace if we keep our minds stayed on Him. Is there anything in your life that you can continually praise God for? When we taste and see that the Lord is good and all that He has done, we know how blessed we are because we take refuge in the Lord. Because we fear Him, we have no lack. He is good to His children and those who put their trust in Him.

My Prayer

Dear Lord,

Please forgive me that I have not always been mindful that my praises of You should always be in my mouth. Please allow me daily to be reminded that my soul duty is to praise You at all times. I have so much to praise You for, yet I let daily stuff get in my way. You are great and powerful and ever watching over me even when I am not mindful of Your presence. Help me this day to give You the praise You deserve, and forgive me of my shortcomings. True praise belongs only to You and You alone.

My Mouth Will Declare Your Praise

O Lord, open my Lips, and my mouth will declare your praise. (Psalm 51:15)

What would happen if you and I didn't have lips and a mouth to give God praise? What kind of world would this world be? What if we were deaf and could not hear and had no mind to comprehend the beauty of this world or if we hand no ability to breathe in the freshness of the air or to see the loveliness of the children God has loaned to us? What if we could not see the oceans so blue or the mountains that literally reach to the clouds? What if we could not hear the morning sounds of the birds giving God glory singing so beautifully with the rising of the morning sun? What if we could not feel the wind blowing with a soft breeze to comfort us? What if we could not see or feel the snow that cleanses the earth each year? What if we could not appreciate the harvest of plenty as the earth provides an abundance of food in every season? What if we could not pick up our toothbrush, or give ourselves a bath, or run and play and enjoy each day as God had given to us? What if there was no night and no time for rest? What would our lives be? What if there were no friendly smiles or caring eyes or hands to comfort our hurts? What if we had no food on our tables or electric lights or air conditioning or automobiles or schools for learning or sites to bury our dead? What if there were no laws of the land and violence was out of control? What if you were left to do what is right in your own eyes? What kind of world would this be? So I end as I begin— what would happen if you and I didn't have lips and a mouth to give God praise?

We say we don't have anything to praise God for. Look around you, and you might discover that everything in the universe was designed by God for our benefit to give Him praise.

My Prayer

Dear Lord,

Give me a broken spirit and a broken and contrite heart, one that You will not despise. Help me to give You praise and honor in all the things You allow me to see, speak, and hear. Help me to walk upright, and let my life reflect Your goodness, Your grace, and Your mercy. Let me love others as You have loved me, and let my life be filled with Your joy. Forgive me of my selfishness and not recognizing You in everything. Purge me, wash me, and incline Your ear to me. Forgive me and cover my sins with Your precious blood. Thank You, Lord, that You allowed me to live in Your universe, to be a part of Your chosen family, making me a joint heir with Your Son, Jesus. You are truly good, awesome in Your ways, and merciful to this piece of clay. Thank You for the loving kindness You have shown to me.

An underserving child,
Evelyn

Make Your Face Shine upon Us

Let the people praise you, O God; let all the people praise you! (Psalm 67:3)

Who are you that the face of God shines upon you, little man, woman, or child? Do you have favor with God, and if so, how would you know it? God blesses us by giving us a good harvest, peace, and children and His own presence in our lives. Have you examined your life lately to see what blessing and honor the Lord has bestowed upon you and your household? God wants to bless all of His people who have acknowledged Him as their personal Savior. There are great rewards in knowing, serving, and loving your Creator, the true and living King of Kings and Lord of Lords and the ultimate ruler of the universe. God keeps us, He guards us and protects us, and He allows His face to shine upon us. When God's face shines upon us, it indicates that God shows favor to His people. When God lifts up His countenance toward His people, it means that God is taking notice of His people and treating them with favor and gives them peace, which means He cares about their total well-being.

May The Lord bless you and keep you.
May The Lord make His face to shine upon you
And be gracious to you;
May The Lord lift up His countenance upon you
And give you peace.
So shall they put my name
Upon the people of Israel.

My Prayer

Dear Lord,

Make Your face to shine upon me today, and do not be ashamed of me today. Let me do nothing to embarrass You today, and let my way be pleasing to You this day. I know there are many days that I have disappointed You and made Your face turn from me in disgust because of my unbecoming behavior. Please forgive me and wash me, clean me up with Your tender mercies and love. Heal my wounds and scars, and make me righteous in Your sight. Thank You for Your word and allowing me see so many wonderful and marvelous things about You. I love You, Lord.

Be gracious to me,
Evelyn

And I Will Bless Them

(Numbers 6:24–27)

Are you praying that God would bless you with a fruitful harvest? Can the rest of the world see Jesus in you? And because of you, will they come to the saving knowledge of Jesus Christ and come to Him and know the true God because of the fruit we have borne. We must remind ourselves daily of whom we are in Him and know who we belong to. Because we are children of God, there ought to be some signs. If He is your father, there should be some resemblance of Him in our lives. Trust in the Lord with all of your heart, and lean not to your own understanding and let Him direct your path.

My Prayer

Dear Lord,

Please let Your face shine upon me today. Keep me from hurt, harm, or danger, and let my words be seasoned with the rich and powerful words of the scriptures. Let me not knowingly plan evil for anyone and keep Your light near so I can see my way through the darkness of each day. Bless me and my family with Your kind presence, and let us be a household that will always worship and honor You. Stay close to our hearts, and let us make decisions for ourselves that are pleasing to You. Forgive us of our sins, and let our hearts be repenting hearts daily. Give us wisdom, and let it always reflect Your goodness, glory, and mercy. Let us not turn away from serving You ever. Be our light and lamp, and keep us saturated, satisfied, and situated in Your word. Thank You, Lord, for the scriptures, for the Savior for salvation, for our struggles, and for Your sustaining grace. Keep me grounded by letting me know that this world is passing away and that all that we have is vanity and fleeing like a bird uncaged. Go with me as I go, and let me lead someone to Your throne of mercy today.

I love You, Lord. Keep me protected in Your mercy and covered like the dew of the morning. Thank You for Your patience with me, and forgive me of all of my hidden sins and bondage. Wash me, and shower me with Your embrace, and love me with Your unconditional love. Thank You, Lord, for Your wisdom in creating me in Your image and in Your likeness. Thank You for choosing me before the foundations of the world to be set apart for Your service. Let me live up to the plans You have for me and to accept what Your plans are towards me. Help me to keep quiet when I want to speak, and when I speak, let my words come from You. Bless me this day and always.

Your humble servant,
Evelyn

Moses Sings unto the Lord

Who is like unto thee, O Lord, among the gods? Who is like thee, glorious in holiness, fearful in praises, doing wonders? (Exodus 15:11)

Our great and sovereign Lord has done such great marvelous and wonderful things in our lives—things that are too great for us to comprehend how we ought to praise Him. Do you let praise ring out in a song, a dance, or a testimony of the goodness of God? Moses had told the children of Israel to fear not, and stand still and see the salvation of the Lord, which He will show you today; for the Egyptians who you have seen today, you shall see them no more forever. For the Lord was with them. God had done great things for the children of Israel, bringing them through the Red Sea on dry land and protecting them by day and by night, leading them in the right direction.

When trouble comes and we cannot see our way, we are reminded of what Moses told the children of Israel when they cried to the Lord: "The Lord shall fight for you, and you shall hold your peace." The question is, can we hold our peace when the storms around us are raging? When our enemies are upon us and our worlds as we know it are turned upside down? When God works on our behalf, our enemies will know who our God is. When we trust Him, God will go before us and behind us and come between us so that our enemies will truly say the Lord is with them. Praise belongs to God alone! He is worthy of all of our praise.

My Prayer

Dear Lord,

When storms are raging in my life and my enemies have surrounded me and when I am fearful and cannot see my way, bring to my mind what You told the children of Israel. You are with me in front and behind, and I am surrounded with all you have promised me. Let me live in Your kingdom, knowing Your protection never leaves me or forsakes me. Let me be reminded always that You show Yourself strongest in my weakness. Help me always depend on You no matter what trial I may face in life. Let me depend on what you know about me, and let me say in my troubles, "I don't know what You are doing, but You know."

Keeping calm always,

Evelyn

The Glories of the Messiah and His Bride

I will make Your Name to be remembered in all generations; therefore the people shall praise you forever and ever. (Psalm 45:17)

Who is the bride of Christ? How can we know that we will enter into His prepared chamber of eternal bliss? How precious are the lives of those who will enter into His eternal rest? Are you dressed and ready for the soon-coming King? How will He greet you, and have you made plans to enter His kingdom? Can you worship and praise Him and bow down at His coming? Will you humble yourself and declare in your heart that He is the King of Kings and the Lord of All? Are you ready? Someday our King will come and receive us to Himself and adorn us with His love and all that He has prepared for believers.

God promises us in Revelation 2:7b, "To him that overcomes will I give to eat of the tree of life which is in the midst of the paradise of God." What a wonderful gift for the bride of Christ to be with the Lord in a place where we will never have to worry about food, sickness, harm, or danger. Look at what God did for His children. He prepared a tree of life for us that will yield twelve kinds of fruit for us each month to keep our spiritual bodies healthy and strong. Are you looking forward to going home to live with Jesus? Have you made the necessary preparations? Are you sure of your salvation? If not, now is a good time to stop and pray and ask Jesus to come into your heart and save you. You may be asking the question, "What I must do to be saved?

Acts 16:31 says, "Believe on the Lord Jesus Christ, and you shall be saved." John 3:16 says, "For God so loved the world, the he gave his only begotten Son, that whosoever believeth in him should not perish, but have everlasting life."

We have everlasting life not by what we have done or our goodness or works but what God did through His Son. His Son laid down His life for us that through His blood we could be saved. Who does that, and how many people would you do that for? Our God is good, and His mercy endures forever.

Our God is mighty to save, and just knowing that is praise. He forgives our mess and declares us righteous in the blood. No wonder the world is confused at the name of Jesus, and only those who belong to the family of God understand this.

My Prayer

Dear Lord,

Please give Your children a burning desire to lead someone to Christ today. Let us be mindful that the world is coming to an end and those who do not know You and believe in Your Son will be lost.

I Will Proclaim the Name of the Lord

Oh praise the greatness of our God! (Deuteronomy 32:3)

We are living in difficult days, and the sinful ways of this world are evil and full of sin, violence, and envy, strife, and open defiance of authority. We are bombarded with evil deeds of filthy trash that is pushed on us and our way of life. The world is an embarrassment to the kingdom of God and His earthly saints, the body of Christ. We sit silently as the world pushes upon us their unrighteousness and the evil that is in their hearts. They make laws that are out of control and against the word of God. We know that these things are wrong, yet we as Christians don't feel that we are strong enough or equipped enough in God's word to stand together to do anything about the evil happenings that are in our world and surrounding our lives. So instead of getting involved and crying out against some of the evil that surrounds us, we just stand back and wait for evil men who do not understand who our God is to change what is ordained from the beginning. Yet while we wait in our comfortable, gated, upscale communities, we sit in silence filling our pockets with greed while we allow men with immoral values, money, evil violence, racial detention, unruly children, immorality, porn, homosexuality, adultery, fornication, and all other principalities of Satan to rise around us.

As believers we are to proclaim the name of the Lord and let our praises ring out in our homes, in our cities, and in the world. The word of God declares that if His people would humble themselves and pray, He would hear from heaven and heal our land. The question on the table today is why aren't the leaders of God's house calling for the church to humble themselves and pray? God's promises are true, and until the people of God get busy calling on Him, we will continue be bothered by the sins that so easily weigh us down. We need to be revived, and it needs to start with us individually. Can you stop right now where you are and ask God to heal our land? Can you or will you start where you are a prayer chain that will reach the world? Can you imagine how all who read this book would stop now and form a pray chain in their community and at some point all other communities would join together praying and fellowshipping together? Could we not as the people of God make a change? Will you now proclaim the name of the Lord and declare His greatness? Could we all proclaim the greatness of our awesome and powerful God who knows each of us by our names? Could we not all ask for the healing of the world? Can we taste and see that the Lord is good and when our prayer goes up, His blessing come down? Many people trust in many things, but we believers trust in the name of the Lord our God.

My Prayer

Dear Lord,

Help me not to be selfish in my prayers, Lord. Help me to see Your world as You see it and pray for all people to come to the saving knowledge of Jesus Christ. It is not Your will that any should perish, and only You will search for the loss until You find them. Give all believers a willing heart and mind to lead people to You, letting them know that You are the way, the truth, and the life. Fill me with Your spirit, and let me be humble and unafraid to share the gospel to loss. Forgive me of failing to share You with others and thinking only of myself and my loved ones. You love the whole world that You gave Your only Son that whoever believes in Him should not perish but have everlasting life. Help me give that life to someone today. And thank You for choosing me to share Your word with the people of Your world. I love You, Lord, and thank You for saving me and giving me eternal life. May I never take for granted what You have done for me, giving up Your life and saving me.

Your servant,
Evelyn

The women said to Naomi; Praise to the Lord, who this day has not left you without a guardian-redeemer. May he become famous throughout Israel? (Ruth 4:14)

Have you ever been depressed, in despair, and wringing your hand with disgust and feeling trouble on every side? Maybe you have lost your way at losing a loved one whom you cannot replace. Maybe you are wondering how God is going to make a way for you, crying out in desperation in agony of how you are going to make it in this world all alone, not knowing where your next meal is coming from or where you will sleep. Weathering the storms of life alone is hard and unpredictable, and you cannot see the light at the end of the tunnel. Your nights are sleepless, and the mind is wondering and untrusting. Yet the God of the universe knows you by name and understands what you are going through. He knows the intent of your heart, and He knows how to bear your burden. The problem is, will we trust Him to see us through. Will we hold on to His garment and not let Him go? Will you seek out His perfect will for your life, and will you trust Him with your whole heart and lean not to your own understanding. These questions and more can be answered through the word of God. You can only get to know Him through His word and be awestruck by what He teaches you.

Naomi was in this kind of situation, but God in His divine wisdom put a daughter in the form of a daughter-in-law named Ruth who would put joy back into her life through her son Obed. He put a kinsman redeemer into her life through Boaz, who married Ruth and took care of them both. God knows our concerns even before we ask, and He is the kind of God who gives us joy, peace, and happiness even in the midst of our storms.

To us He has given His Son as our precious Redeemer and Savior. How good He is that He has looked beyond our faults and seen our very needs. Jesus is our Redeemer who loved us and shed His precious blood for us so we would not be lost. He laid down His life for us and presents us faultless before His Father. I don't know about you, but I feel worthless and undeserving of what He did for me. There is nothing I have that I can repay Him with for His goodness, mercy, and love.

My Prayer

Dear Lord,

You are good, gracious, and kind. You are full of mercy and grace that You considered me a little piece of clay, and You formed me to be Your child. There is nothing in me that I can say or do to repay You for Your generosity toward me. Forgive me for not recognizing sooner this wonderful, awesome, and rich mercy You have shown to me. Thank You for saving me and preparing a place for me in Your kingdom. I am so undeserving of Your loving kindness. Thank You, dear Lord, that You are giving me eternal life in Your kingdom, forgetting and forgiving all my horrific sins. If I could praise You the rest of my days, it would not be enough to give You all the glory You deserve. I am honored to be Your child; I am honored to bow my knees before You and honored to be Your servant who will cast my crowns before You. Thank You, merciful God, that You are truly worth of all praise, glory, and honor. You are truly worthy to be crowned Kings of Kings and Lord of Lords. Fill me and wash me with Your Holy Spirit, that I may grow to be more like You each day. May I represent Your kingdom well in this sinful world. I love You, great and mighty God. Be with me always, and let Your light shine in me so that all will see that I belong to You. May Your peace be mine today and peace also to all Your children on the earth who are called by Your name.

Honored to be Your child,
Evelyn

About the Author

Evelyn Reid is a twenty-year cancer survivor who chose not to take chemotherapy. She is the author of *Cancer: a Sentence to Live* and has done extensive studies in natural and homeopathic medicine. Her background includes professional modeling, radio, television, and public speaking. Mrs. Reid is a former a professor of women's studies at Crossroads Institute of Biblical Studies in Macon, Georgia, and currently hosts a television show called *Getting Healthy with Evelyn Reid,* which can be seen on YouTube. Reid works with Global Faith Alliance, which does missions in third-world countries. Evelyn is married. Her husband, Dr. Donald M. Reid, is pastor of the Aletheia Baptist Church and president of Crossroads Institute of Biblical Studies; they are the parents of one daughter, Leni Shontae', and one grandson, Evan Donald Simmons.

Daring to be different and taking the time to get to know the God of the Bible can be a challenge. What can cause a mere mortal to desire to know the living God? It may be trouble, loss of a loved one, financial difficulties, etc., or just a passion to know more about Him.

When depression, hardship, loneliness, or trouble happen on every hand or take control of your heart, you may want to have an intimate relationship with God. That's what happened to Evelyn Reid. Her desire to know her God in an up-close and personal way led her to do the studies on praise and worship. Worshiping God is essentially an audience of one. It requires one with a desire and with the intent to know Him more. What she realized in taking and spending this time with the Lord made her realize that no matter how much time spent in the word, there is still more to know. His vast being is too wonderful to know everything about Him. However, the joy of discovery is both awesome and amazing.

Getting into God's word can be a wonderful and beautiful experience for anyone. People who know their God can do great and wonderful things for the kingdom. Hopefully this study will empower you to put your trust in God and worship Him more intently. May God richly bless you as you give Him His rightful place in your life.

Printed in the United States
By Bookmasters